D1106608

THE INEVITABLE ENCOUNTER

Other books by
EDWARD L. R. ELSON

ONE MOMENT WITH GOD
AMERICA'S SPIRITUAL RECOVERY
AND STILL HE SPEAKS

PREACHING FOR TODAY

THE INEVITABLE
ENCOUNTER

by
EDWARD L. R. ELSON
The National Presbyterian Church
Washington, D.C.

WM. B. EERDMANS PUBLISHING COMPANY
GRAND RAPIDS, MICHIGAN

To the members

of

THE NATIONAL PRESBYTERIAN CHURCH

for whom affection deepens
with the passing of the years

PREFACE

Much has been said of late about the softening of Christian character and the diluting of the Christian witness. Observers give much attention to what they regard as the shallow, superficial and uncertain expressions of Christianity today. Certainly in this era, when church membership is at an all-time high, there are multitudes of people who are merely over the doorstep into the household of faith. All that lies before them should be growth in grace and in comprehension of Christian truth. On the one hand, there are massive minds at the theological summit; and on the other hand, churches full of immature Christians and amateur theologians. There is a great gap between the new theologian and the new Christian. The Church itself is a challenging arena for evangelism and education.

Yet there is another aspect to modern Christianity. The days through which we have lived have been heroic days. In hosts of individuals I have seen the spirit of Christ revealed as emphatically and sometimes as dramatically as in any period of Church history. I have seen it in prisoners in concentration camps, in soldiers in combat, in the refugees whom my parishioners have established in new lives in America. I have seen it in heroic individuals such as Dr. John D. Hayes, my associate in the ministry of the National Presbyterian Church, to whom I have alluded in the first chapter of this book. I have seen it in that guardian of American freedom and that exponent of the Christian home and religious education, J. Edgar Hoover — constantly crusading in the face of ridicule and disdain from those who would make the easy compromise. I have seen it in John Foster Dulles, who carried Christian principles into international affairs to the point where the chief criticism of both his friends and his adversaries was that he "moralized" too much! There at the crossroads of history he stood through stormy years, loyal to the faith into which he was born, which nourished his ideas and sustained his actions. I have seen it in Walter H. Judd, a consecrated physician taking into the halls of Congress the same Christian dedication he took to the mission fields in China. I have seen it in Dwight D. Eisenhower, who absorbed for all of us the vulgarities and indignities of Khrushchev at their last meeting and on many another occasion has stood for the hard right against the easier expediency. Not the least, I have seen the spirit of Christ expressed day by day in the lives of unnamed government workers whose duties are performed as "unto the Lord," whose integrity, industry, sterling character and patriotic devotion are unexcelled anywhere and in any age. I have seen the spirit of Christ in physicians, lawyers, teachers, tradesmen, diplomats, Congressmen, jurists and military leaders. Only a vital personal encounter with the living God, through Jesus Christ, sustains these men. I do not despair for the Church today. In men who respond to God's offer in the Gospel, there is hope.

Since World War II I have had the awesome responsibility and the high privilege of ministering in one of America's most historic churches. Such a place sometimes can be frightening; it is always humbling. Washington is a microcosm of the United States. It is more than a capital city. Decisions made by men in this place affect the destiny of all mankind. Here, too, we meet and minister to people from every nation. The Gospel needed by men working in such a place, grappling with agonizing decisions, is the unchanging Gospel of redeeming love made known in our Lord Jesus Christ. Preaching to people in all walks of life and in a variety of vocations, I have discovered that if you preach the Gospel of our Lord Jesus Christ you will get home to the needs of statesmen, diplomats, and politicians. For all men are in need of Christ.

From the beginning of my ministry I have endeavored in my preaching to express the classical evangelical witness of the Holy Catholic Church Reformed. While my roots have been in a conservative environment I have had extensive graduate study in a liberal university. Throughout the years I have sought to be familiar with the emerging schools of theological thought but to refrain from becoming typed as a "disciple of a disciple," hoping instead to remain in the classical tradition, free from transient fads. I have not thought it my duty to shock or to entertain a congregation. Nor have I adopted an overly sophisticated style. Excessive sophistication begets homiletical exhibitionism, too often a display of the preacher rather than a declaration of the Gospel. For the Gospel first, last and always is given to us — not conjured by us. I have prayed that I might present timely messages on the timeless Gospel.

No man lives to himself in his study, in his pulpit, or his daily encounters. He lives and works with others in daily fellowship, thinking their thoughts after them. Ideas migrate from man to man, and from generation to generation. There is a reciprocity of theme and structure between preachers, but a naturalness and a newness in each individual preacher. I am in debt to a whole "cloud of witnesses," past and present, with whom I have had fellowship and whose works have helped make me what I am. Many sermons have been preached on Paul's shipwreck as recorded in The Acts 27, but nowhere have I seen the interpretation given to it which I reflect in the chapter "Standing Up to a Crisis." The sermon "The Church and the New Frontiers" was preached on the Sunday following the inauguration of President John F. Kennedy.

Each year I preach several series of sermons. The sermons in this instance are all topical. The one thing which the following sermons have in common is that they were all preached in the National Presbyterian Church in Washington and have been selected because they have in some special way met the needs of the people who heard them. When asked by the publishers of PREACHING FOR TODAY to contribute to their series, I was pleased to make these messages available in permanent form.

EDWARD L. R. ELSON

The Little Narrows
Cape Breton, Nova Scotia
August 1, 1962

CONTENTS

xi

I

THE HIGHER WITNESS

JESUS made four promises to His disciples. He assured them:

First, they would have joy.
Second, they would possess a serene peace.
Third, they would have dynamic power.
Fourth, they would get into trouble.

All four of these promises were fulfilled. The disciples had an exuberant, outgoing joy. They did possess a peace of soul no changing scene could disturb. They had such power that men said, "These are they who have turned the world upside down." They did get into trouble – all kinds of trouble.

Christian discipleship has never come cheaply. It has never been easy to be a Christian. Only men of robust faith and sturdy convictions stand up when the real test comes.

This truth is emphasized in Jesus' commissioning words to His disciples. He predicted that they would be confronted by opposition, that they would be as sheep among wolves. He warned that they would be persecuted by fanatics and intolerant religious bigots who would deliver them up to the councils and would scourge them in the synagogues. He said that for their loyalty to Him they might be hauled up before totalitarian rulers – would be brought before kings and governors. So acute would the tensions between Christ and anti-Christ become that even the intimate family circle would be broken. One thing would be certain: they would meet general hostility everywhere. But He gave them a glorious promise — "... he that endureth to the end shall be saved" (Matthew 10:22).

Then later, when the risen Christ met His disciples on the hillside in Galilee, He declared, "Ye shall be witnesses unto me" (Acts 1:8). The word "witness" as understood in English does not really convey what Christ intended His disciples to understand. This is a luminous word which, when discarding its ordinary meanings and our feeble translation, walks forth in the dazzling glory of a revealing transliteration and says not merely, "Ye shall be witnesses," but rather, "Ye shall be martyrs — my martyrs." This word tracks a daring pathway when we follow it through apostolic Christianity.

The disciples were to shine for Christ, but soon they discovered that they were to burn as they shone. They did go forth upon their radiant mission. They were martyrs of His life, His deeds, and of the words which He had said. They were martyrs of His sufferings. Hence they were prepared to be martyrs of His glory. They made their martyrdom a proof of His resurrection. They were so certain that Jesus Christ had persisted beyond death and was alive and with them forevermore that they were ready to die for Him.

It cost a terrific price to be a disciple of Jesus Christ in apostolic days. Disciples then did not live in a congenial and comfortable atmosphere. At the beginning the whole world was not only inhospitable, but positively hostile to them. A crimson stream runs from the cross to the glory of eternity. Paul, the apostle, bore witness to his call to be a martyr both of the things which he had already seen and of the things to be revealed. John, the revelator, on the Island of Patmos, saw Jesus, the faithful martyr, "the firstborn of the dead," and then testified: "unto him that loved us, and washed us from our sins in his own blood, and hath made us kings and priests unto God and his Father; to him be glory and dominion for ever and ever... Behold, he cometh with clouds..." (Revelation 1:5-7).

But what clouds? Not fleecy and foamy clouds but clouds of glory. The writer beholds clouds of martyrs: "Wherefore seeing we also are compassed about with so great a crowd of martyrs" (Hebrews 12:1). Here is the figure of a vast amphitheater with the multitude of saints of the ages past looking down upon those who in life's arena run the race for Christ now. There are clouds of martyrs. Little wonder that the writer of the Apocalypse heralds the appearance of the "souls of them that were beheaded for martyrdom unto Jesus, and for the word of God, and which had not worshipped the beast...neither had received his mark upon their foreheads or in their hands" (Revelation 20:4). "These are they," says the seer, "which came out of great tribulation, and have washed their robes, and made them white in the blood of the lamb" (Revelation 7:14).

It is not sadism to remind ourselves that our Christian forebears gave their lives that we might have the faith we now sometimes take so lightly. Our push-button, automated, gadget-ridden generation, abounding in luxuries and creature comforts, may well reflect upon the price of discipleship, not only in generations past but in our own day. For the real apostolic succession is not so much by ordination or creed or church, although all of these are important and necessary, as it is by apostolic succession of martyrdom — "Ye shall be my martyrs."

The true successors of the "glorious company of the apostles and the goodly fellowship of the prophets," as the Te Deum sings, are those whose souls are rooted in costly discipleship. From Stephen the first martyr, with eyes fixed upon Jesus, through the whole company of the apostles, save one, through the flaming witnesses of several centuries, runs the story of glorious faith: Blandina, the martyr maiden, who could only cry, "We do nothing that is evil"; Ponticus, only fifteen years of age, dying for his risen Lord; Ponthinus the Bishop of Lyons, giving his all at the age of ninety; blessed Polycarp of Smyrna who, when asked to renounce Christ, testified before his tormentors, "Four score and six years have I been His servant and He has done me no wrong. How then can I blaspheme my King who has saved me?"

In his helpful book *The Hour Has Come*, Dr. A. Ray Jordan reminds us that in the early days of persecution the worst sentence given a devotee of Christ was not death but *damnatus ad metalla*. This sentence banished the Christians to the mines of Numidia. Here they were subjected to indescribable horror. On arrival in Africa, these strange exiles were first brutally whipped. Then, as they moved through the rock valleys to Saigus the blazing sun burned their bodies. Next they were marked on the brow with a hot iron as cattle are branded. Their chains were shortened to bend their bodies for life. The descriptions of what took place remind us of the concentration camps of recent times. Indescribable forms of brutality were visited upon these poor souls as with lamp and pick they were put to work in the dark tunnels.

In Numidia the life in Christ was not extinguished, but shone for all time in bright incandescence. Little prayers and inscriptions were left on the walls. One word is written so often that it must have been the theme of every Christian condemned to this place. Like a great electric sign it spoke to every passer-by. The word was *vita* — "life." Even in the mine of Numidia Christians had life and they had joy in life because they knew God as Jesus revealed Him. They thought of Him, loved Him, lived with Him, died for Him, and lived eternally. This is the open secret of all Christians.

We must never forget the terrific cataclysm of the early Christian era with its ebbing and flooding tide of imperial persecution, black-marked by the names of Nero, Domitian, Marcus Aurelius, Septimius Severus, Valerian and Diocletian. Indelibly in our memories there must be preserved the price of discipleship through the centuries. Ever and again we must hear the testimony to Christian truth in the lives of Huss and Wycliffe; in the careers of Livingstone, Carey, Morrison, and others. "Ye shall be my martyrs."

Although the fury spent itself, and suffering at times was not the cost of discipleship, there have been recurring epochs when the kindling torch still burned here and there. Mission lands in our own day have not been alien to its awesome light. There was Simcox, and Hodge, of the boxer days in China. You may read on the wall of the Y.M.C.A. Building in Shanghai the names of scores of Chinese Christians who gave their love unto death for the sake of Christ. You may even have the privilege of meeting face to face those who bear in their bodies the mark of the Lord Jesus Christ. There was Robert Chung, a friend of mine in student days, tortured by the Japanese military for his witness in Korea; or Roger Cumberland, stabbed in the back by infuriated opponents for his witness in Iran; or Ralph Hall, one of the missionaries of the Presbyterian Board of National Missions who was strung up by drunken cowboys in one of our western states but who gave such convincing Christian testimony and exhibited such courage that his would-be executioners spared his life and were converted. There was John Hayes, for some time after World War II my colleague on the staff of the National Presbyterian Church, who returned to China, the land of his birth, as a missionary, only to be arrested by the Communists, cruelly brainwashed and tortured, and threatened five times with execution, who testified "determined to tell the truth and to be true to Christ." Even in our generation these have been —

> Comrades of the souls supreme,
> Conscripts of a mighty dream,
> Brave souls who took the perilous trail,
> And felt the vision would not fail.

"Ye shall be my martyrs."

The great Church historian, Kenneth Latourette, has called the century ending in 1914 "the greatest century of the Church." The period since 1914 he has entitled "Advance Through Storm."

There has hardly been an age when it has been truer that the blood of the martyrs has been the seed of the Church. "Ye shall be my witnesses" even to martyrdom has been dramatized repeatedly in our own generation. In all the heroism of World War II with its incredible victories and individual gallantry there is nothing more magnificent than the heroism of the Church. Roman Catholic and Protestant men of God did not cower or cringe or whine. It was not the universities nor the press nor the politicians that stood up against the paganism of the Nazis, but as Dr. Einstein reminded us, the religious leaders alone revealed a competency to deal with the new brutalities and to protest against the infamies of the new pagan order.

When the Nazi butcher at Athens was about to execute a fresh crop of hostages, he was confronted by the bishop of Athens, who protested the legality and the morality of the actions. Handing him a paper, he said, "Here is a list of persons whom you could shoot without having society suffer immeasurably." "Show me the list," said the officer. At the head of the list was the name of the bishop himself, and there followed all the names of the Greek clergy. Such a sacrificial offer dazed even the S.S. officer, and the demand for hostages was abated. "Ye shall be my martyrs."

One day the magnificent Bishop Berggrav of Norway was hauled up before Quisling, whom he had been outwitting. "You deserve to be beheaded," the puppet ruler cried when Berggrav called him to account. "Well, here I am," the Bishop said calmly, and Quisling was thwarted.

On the day in 1945 when I had completed my investigation of the imprisoned clergy at Dachau Concentration Camp, there occurred a singularly humbling experience. At this most infamous of all concentration camps 2,448 ministers of religion had been imprisoned, of which number more than 1,000 had died there. When I was about to leave and was saying farewell to some of the Protestant pastors, there stood before me the Rev. Nicholas Padt, the distinguished former pastor of the Reformed Church at Zutphen, Holland. With his tattered shirt held together by a single button, his ragged trousers sustained by an ancient pair of suspenders, a pair of unmated shoes protruding at the bottom, and with a little bundle of rags under his arm, he was preparing to go to the disinfecting booth. After due processing he was placed with a group of other Dutch prisoners to be returned to Holland.

In the course of our conversation this fifty-nine-year-old hero of the Church pounded his fist on the table and exclaimed, "I have not done one day's work for the Third Reich in two years!" Somewhat startled, I inquired, "Pastor Padt, every prisoner whom I have questioned has had to work to stay alive, and some who labored perished nevertheless; how does it happen that you have not had to work?" "Well," said he, "early in my career as a prisoner I deliberately developed a reputation for decrepitude, malingering, and worthlessness, so that — when the S.S. guards came for a work detail — they simply slammed me on the floor, kicked me in the belly and the ribs, and left me lying there. Then, when they had gone, I gathered myself up and went about my own affairs." "Ye shall be my witnesses." Oh, no! It is more than that. "Ye shall be my martyrs," even in our generation.

When I think of Pastor Padt and others like him, who were fighting the diabolical neo-paganism of our generation and the new barbarism, kicked in the belly and the ribs, but refusing to submit, I am ashamed, starkly ashamed that my religion has cost me so little. I cannot restrain the feeling of an enormous debt to these Christians who, at cost of great suffering, kept alive the Christian witness in their part of the world. They were ready when the Master called: "Ye shall be my martyrs."

Today we hear these words in the comfort and beauty of our own churches. We salute the past, but fail to live as crusading Christians in the present. Christianity began and survived with a passion and power for this kind of witness. Men, women, and young people came under the spell of something supernatural which utterly possessed them, and to which they gave themselves completely. Nothing is more pathetic, tragic, and disappointing than an individual or a church, completely objective and detached, that has lost the thrill of a great cause and is unable or unwilling to bear witness with courage. When the Church becomes decadent, it tries to save itself, forgetting the essence of the gospel, "Whosoever will save his life shall lose it; but whosoever shall lose his life for my sake and the gospel's, the same shall save it" (Mark 8:35). We shall never be able to challenge or overcome the engulfing tide of paganism that sweeps over our world unless we build our faith upon a sure foundation of this costly apostolic faith and passion. A *dilettante* church cannot hope to win a world. Only by willingness to pay the price can we do so. It takes a rugged and robust faith. It requires a sturdy brand of Christian witnessing.

In his anniversary address to the National Presbyterian Church, Dr. Charles Malik called everyone to heart-searching when he said:

> Beyond every burden and care, the Christian has his own soul to worry about. Oh, yes, he is honest and upright, he works hard, he reads the Bible, he meditates on the saints, he has his times of profound prayer and retreat to the depths, he lives an active Church life, he takes a humble part in the stirring spiritual movements of the day, he is alive to the problems of the world, he is as good and solid a citizen as any other person, and, above all, he develops ulcers, those peculiar *stigmata* of our age! But, is he the master of his own passions? How much does he know the living power of God in his own life — that power which is much more than the *daimon* of Socrates which only warns and forbids, that power which also directs and constitutes and provides? Is he at peace with himself? Is he true to himself? Is he true to Christ? How much does Christ come to his rescue exactly in time? In his daily wrestlings with the devil, does he spit in his face and trample his head under foot — not in his own

power, but always in the power of the Cross? Has he forgiven
his brother — really forgiven him? Is all rancour and resentment washed away by the blood of Christ? How else can he
hope for the forgiveness of God of which he stands in such
desperate need?[1]

Today we hear these words, "Ye shall be my martyrs," and we
misunderstand. We think it says —

"Ye shall be — my parochial errand boys, flitting about for the
Lord.

"Ye shall be — my theological debating society, God's defenders
of the faith, everlastingly contending, but never discerning His
presence and truth.

"Ye shall be — my parish busybodies, fussing about trivialities
and missing the glory of the risen Christ.

"Ye shall be — my pew occupants, displacing so much space in
the church — unresponsive to the Master's urgent claims.

"Ye shall be — my calendar charters, tracing hypothetic pre-
dictions but neglecting the work of the Lord.

"Ye shall be — my fifty-seven varieties of noon-day religions in
service clubs with all their animated wind and sustained ballyhoo.

"Ye shall be — my current events analysts, analyzing events
instead of proclaiming God's great event.

"Ye shall be — my preachers, uttering dead words rather than
witnessing to the living Word."

But our Lord commissioned us to none of these. "Ye shall be my
witnesses — martyrs, my representatives of the Son of God, who
stopped not at a cross, and who calls His disciples to take up a
cross of sacrifice and follow Him."

Not many of us are privileged to suffer and die for Christ. But
all of us are called to let our light shine brightly here, to witness
to the glory of Christ, to give generously out of the bounty of our
resources to His Church, that Christ's Church be not ashamed,

---

[1]Quotation taken from Dr. Malik's recent book, *Christ and Crisis* (Grand
Rapids: Eerdmans, 1962), pp. 95-6.

but empowered; that the wonder and glory of the gospel be known everywhere.

When tempted by complacent conformity to custom and tradition and the enslaving habits of the mob mind, we in our up-holstered, air-conditioned, luxury-loving age need to hear again and understand these words, "Ye shall be my martyrs," and sing from the depths —

> *Faith of our fathers! Living still . . .*
> *We will be true to Thee till death.*

2

THE EVERLASTING ARMS

T HE giant eagle was familiar to the ancient world. Its image was carried as a talisman before the legions of Rome. Today the eagle is mounted on the top of our flagstaffs and is part of the great seal of the United States, a symbol of triumphant righteousness.

The eagle is a Biblical bird. In the mood of a poet living close to nature, the author of the book of Deuteronomy portrays the picture of an eagle teaching her young to fly (Chapter 32, verse 11). The eagle first stirs up the nest and tosses the young one out into the expanse of space to test his pinions. As the fledgling hurtles through the great reaches of air and space and seems about to meet destruction in the abyss, the giant mother swoops down from the heights, catches the young one upon her body and bears him aloft. The process is repeated over and over again until the eaglet becomes certain that wherever he goes and whatever he experiences there is a supporting love beneath him.

With this concept still in mind, Moses reminds the people of the saving power of God. How fortunate for this ancient people, he says, that divine care has ever been between them and disaster. They have been taught and guided, reinforced and redeemed by God who is ever with them. The passage ends triumphantly with the familiar words of our text, "The eternal God is our refuge, and underneath are the everlasting arms."

A profound truth to be seen here is that there is an everlasting reality underneath everything. When that which is

11

underneath is studied, its real significance becomes evident. Surfaces never reveal true meanings. There is something ever-lasting underneath the cosmos, underneath nature, underneath history, and underneath human personality.

Underneath the cosmos there is something everlasting. From the tiniest atom and its components to the vastest galaxy beyond this universe there is order and law. Beneath all the order and law is intelligence. We cannot segregate it, define it, or reproduce it. It is simply there. Years ago, Sir James Jeans said reality, or that essence which is at the heart of things, appears more like a great idea, what we call spirit, than anything else. Joseph Kaplan, chairman of the Geophysical Year Committee, asserts that there is a supreme mind at the center of things with which the mind of man seeks communion, and that prayer is the most natural and elevating exercise of man. There it is . . . a vast spirit underneath it all. There is something underneath the cosmos.

Underneath nature there is something everlasting. There is always something far deeper in nature than can be measured, attested, or classified scientifically. There is something deeper than we can perceive. Here is the rose we take into our hands so appreciatively yet familiarly, but underneath it is not only the seed that perished in the darkness to give it life, not only the little shoot that showed above the ground, but a strange miracle we cannot fathom or dispute. Life and beauty are there. A man can make an automobile or an atomic bomb, but he can neither discover the nature nor reproduce the material which makes one petal of that rose. In nature there is always something underneath.

Underneath history there is something everlasting. Man makes history and participates in it, but history belongs to Another — a Divine Being. History seems to be an unending story of human folly and wickedness, of human grandeur and sacrifice, of heights of nobility and depths of ignominy and shame, but there is always something beneath it, the discovery of which gives coherence and significance. History moves with a purpose. Hidden deep beneath the surface is a Mind and Will at work. Behind the heroism, the majesty, and magnanimity of individuals, God is at work in history.

I remember a Scottish doctor discussing the British debacle at Dunkirk in World War II. He could not understand why it happened nor how the United Kingdom could be preserved from invasion and ultimate destruction. But he said, "If the people of the Islands have yet a service to render to humanity, God will lead, direct, and empower them." In that episode there were, in fact, hidden and inexplicable factors even now not fully understood. God is a God of history. History will ever remain an insoluble enigma until we see the world as the area of God's redeeming activity, in which men of every race, color, nation, and creed are equal, the law of which is love, and the Ruler of which is God. Once you see that, you see love and sacrifice for what they are — the extension and reproduction of the Cross of Christ in every place and age. There is something everlasting underneath history.

And underneath human personality there is something everlasting. Many books have been written about personality, but nobody has yet given a satisfactory, completely understandable definition of what it is. Though we know what the chemical components of the body are, we know that persons are more than a certain arrangement of chemical elements. Personality is more than lime and salt and potash and some other chemicals. Personality is more than the circulatory, nervous, or respiratory systems precisely organized and functioning efficiently. We know that our physical body changes over the years but we always remain the same identifiable person. There is an underneath to personality.

That which is most real in individuals, which makes them most distinctive, which makes each living person an unduplicated entity in all this universe — that which really makes you what you are and me what I am and distinguishes each of us from every other being in the whole universe — whatever that is cannot be assessed, evaluated, or attested by scientific formulas and processes. And yet, that is the most distinctive thing about us — that mysterious, undefinable element called personality. And whatever that unique, distinguishing quality is, we may be sure it will cause us to be known and to know each other on the other side of death, when the "mortal puts on immortality." There is an underneath to personality.

What a thrilling lesson we have here. The highest truth we can learn is that what is underneath is the everlasting, the permanent, the eternal. We cannot comprehend the everlasting; we can only apprehend it — touch it, feel its quality, realize its nature, open our lives to it. A sunset and a rose are both realities in human experience. We can apprehend them, but we can never fully comprehend them. The underneath of reality which is everlasting is the invisible — "the things which are seen are temporal; but the things which are not seen are eternal" (2 Corinthians 4:18). This gives us a more Christian view of death. Paul talked about the distinction between a natural body and a spiritual body. And long ago, in Ecclesiastes, it was written, "Then shall the dust return to the earth as it was: and the spirit shall return unto God who gave it" (Ecclesiastes 12:7). The reality about every one of us is the "everlasting underneath."

"Underneath are the everlasting arms." Whose arms are underneath? Well, the first phrase of that text is "The eternal God is thy refuge." Then comes our text, "underneath are the everlasting arms." Life's underneath and everlasting are in reality the very arms of God.

How life is lifted and strengthened when we lay hold on this truth! With the arms we reach and stretch. God reaches right down into our human hearts and lives — right into the depths of things. It is with the arms that work is done. It is with the arms we welcome and embrace one another — and with the arms the thankful father gathers the prodigal to his heart. So do the arms of God embrace His children — and sometimes they wrestle with them as the hymn "O God of Bethel" reminds us. The arms that reach, that work, that wrestle, that love, that forgive, and that hold — these are underneath life. They are often beneath us when we least suspect it and they never leave us nor forsake us, either in time or eternity.

"Underneath are the everlasting arms." It is so with you. During your defeats, your complacency, your obstinacy, your moral roving, your failures, there has been something underneath. The everlasting arms have been there when you have been least conscious of them. They are there now. They are there when, like the little eagle, you go crashing to what seems like certain destruction. They are there when you are positive you have nothing to show for your life. They are there while you live, when you die, and through all eternity after dying. The everlasting arms are under the cosmos, under nature, under history, under personality — under the self-invisible. They reach out even to the far country — to love us back to the Father's heart. They never leave us nor forsake us.

Those of us who remember another generation will recall the socialist leader, Eugene V. Debs, who for varied reasons spent considerable time in prison. During one of his periods in prison an old Negro lifer lay dying, and in his delirium he kept calling for his mammy. Debs asked to see him. When he entered the hospital cell he bent low over the old Negro, then gathered him up in his arms and sang, "Swing low, sweet chariot, Comin' for to carry me home; Swing low ... Comin' for to carry me home." By and by the chariots of the eternal Lord swept down and carried him off. And as he went, the old Negro said, "I knew you'd come, Mammy, I knew you'd come." In life, at death, and beyond, there is reality underneath.

This we know; I say, we *know*. We have seen in history God's everlasting arms that are underneath all time and eternity

— the arms of Jesus Christ on a cross — embracing the whole of humanity, eternally saving men, eternally proclaiming everlasting redemptive love. We can never feel that there is nothing underneath, that we are alone, unsupported, weak, bereft, when we have seen the Cross. There, once for all is revealed, once for all is proclaimed — Love laying down its life "a ransom for many." At the heart of things is redemptive love. It is a love that will not let us go. Across the centuries comes the message, "Lo, I am with you alway" (Matthew 28:20) — even unto the end of the end. "Underneath are the everlasting arms."

Eternal God, who art our refuge and strength, we thank Thee for the arms that reach out to gather in all Thy children, and that even now embrace us. Teach us day by day this truth. Make us good enough and great enough and strong enough for tomorrow's tasks.

Through Jesus Christ, our Lord.

Amen

"I have called you friends."
John 15:15

3

JESUS THE FRIEND

JESUS of history is inescapable. We see Him so clearly striding across the Galilean countryside — a strong young man, sun-tanned, ruddy-faced, with flowing hair and beard, with horny hands, protruding chest, and sturdy muscles. Entering into the life of His people, this winsome young man tugs a fisherman's net, or yanks a boat up out of the water, while He reveals a great truth. He puts His hand to a farmer's plow and quietly tells a parable. He jests and plays with little children. He talks with the infirm and the aged. He calls forth healing faith in the afflicted. He speaks words of forgiveness to sinners. He reads the Scriptures in the synagogues, preaches on street corners, addresses vast throngs in nature's amphitheater, talks in the market places, excites first curiosity and then censorship from religious leaders.

He calls men to follow Him. He appeals to a dozen men to concentrate their talents and energies on His message and mission. For several years they walk with Him. They are fishermen, a tax collector, a politician, men with doubts and fears and flaws. Very human they are, but also very strong. Their counterparts may be found in any land in any age. They travel and they talk with Him. They hear Him speak quiet truths not spoken to the throng. There is between them an intimacy and a comradeship which come only to men who live and work close to one another day by day. They rejoice at His acclamation, thrill at His miracles, sorrow in His rejection.

17

Toward the end of Jesus' public career He began to define the relationship He was to have with them. He related that just as He and the Father were one, so were they one with Him. As branches cannot produce fruit without the vine, neither could they produce the fruits of the Spirit without Him. "Greater love hath no man than this, that a man lay down his life for his friends. You are my friends..." (John 15:13, 14). Soon He was to go out to a lonely hill and demonstrate that truth.

In the past the relationship had been that of master and serv-ant, of teacher and pupil. It is now transformed into that service which is perfect freedom; for the disciples are taken into their Master's confidence as friends, to share all of His life in and with God. "Henceforth I call you not servants... but I have called you friends; for all things that I have heard of my Father I have made known unto you... that whatsoever you shall ask of the Father in my name, he may give it you" (John 15:15, 16).

"I have called you friends."

The essence of friendship is in loving rather than being loved, in giving rather than receiving, in spending one's self for the friend. A friend has all there is of us. The Anglo-Saxon deriva-tion is from *fre'en* — "free man" — meaning the man who has the run of our house. One's heart and mind are utterly open to the friend. In friendship the interior life is common property. There is trust and loyalty, a completeness and a oneness that can never be shattered. Jesus said, "I have called you friends."

Then He went out to die on a cross. And that friendship, though interrupted for three days, was not destroyed. The Friend came again. The intimacy was restored on the same level and in the same richness as before.

A woman standing before the mystery of a vacated grave hears Him say, "Mary." She does not touch Him or even seek for further evidence. In the glow of restored friendship she hurries back to town to tell the good news to the disciples.

That night ten men assemble in the familiar rendezvous — the upper room. The doors are shut. Then they hear His familiar voice: "Peace be unto you" (John 20:19). The Friend has entered — so vivid, so real, so unmistakable in identification. They go and shout to the world, "The Lord is risen!"

When one who was not there heard, he held up his hands in horror. "Never," said Thomas. "That is impossible! What evidence do you have? Are you victims of hysteria? You have yielded to the credulity of the women. At any rate you can't fool me."

Then came the next Sunday evening when eleven men, including Thomas, were in the same old room. The doors were shut. There was a deep longing in each man's heart for some certification. The mood was expectant. Then came the Friend. They were aware of a Presence, and they heard the salutation, "Peace be unto you." It was the Lord. To Thomas He addressed Himself: "Thomas, reach out your hand, touch my side, feel my hands — be not faithless, but believing." Thomas was so overwhelmed by the presence of the Friend that his heart bounded and his voice shouted, "My Lord and my God!" It was not by touch, not by feeling, not by physical data, for there is no evidence that Thomas felt the body. It was simply the authentic presence of the Friend in personal encounter.

Two disciples walk along the Emmaus road, conversing with one who, though at first a stranger, addresses them so intimately and with such assurance that they are drawn to invite him to dine with them. Later, in the quietness of a meal, He is disclosed as the Friend whom they had known before that cruel Friday. "Did not our heart burn within us, while he talked with us by the way?" (Luke 24:32). The Presence, the reality of the Friend, was validated in their common walk and work.

Thus Jesus was establishing this enduring, this indestructible friendship. He came to those who had known Him, loved Him, listened to Him, talked with Him, obeyed Him. He came to them in all their weakness and in their strength. For forty days, to individuals and to groups as large as several hundred, in at least eleven recorded episodes, He made Himself known beyond all doubt. He was establishing the friendship in the unseen depths of personality, where friendship must always be set — in the hidden things not measurable nor attestable — in ideas, in ideals, in principles, in the spirit, in the warmth of emotion, in the inner life, in the dedication and discipline of the will. He was planting the reality of the friendship where it belonged — in the unseen but living reality of personality. Then He went out of some men's sight in order to be near all men — to be the Friend of all believing men in all ages thereafter.

Jesus has never ceased to be that Friend. To all who will hear He says, "I have called you friends." "Come unto me... and I will give you rest" (Matthew 11:28). What He was to those men He would be to all who seek Him. He is perpetually contemporaneous. He is today what He was to His disciples in those first days following the first Easter.

Men went out to live for Him and testify for Him in the conviction that this Friend was alive and with them. They crossed the highest hill, forged the swiftest stream, sailed the wildest sea, suffered imprisonment, torture, and death for this Friend until the message of salvation and the permanent reality of the Friend's life in their lives finally conquered the old pagan world.

And all of the disciples, save one, died a violent death, certain that in life or in death they would never be separated from this Friend. Men do not suffer for an idle dream. Men do not gladly die for an empty hallucination. Jesus was alive, vivid, real to them — an abiding Friend. They were inseparable. The divine mediation for all time was to be in and through this living Christ — this Divine One who is identical with the Jesus some men knew in the flesh.

It is harder to disprove the reality of this friendship than to prove it. For every time men have opened their hearts to Him, given heed to His commands, yielded their lives to His will, He has come "out of the everywhere" into personal life.

This Friend comes to us not so much by argument as by experience. Jack Wyrtzen, a young man in World War II and now a director of the Word of Life Fellowship, tells how the Friend came to him.

> During the first nineteen years of my life I often was lonely and discouraged. I wondered what life was all about, what made us tick, what was the answer to the riddle of life, where we came from and where we were going. Then, at the age of nineteen, while in the United States Army, my buddy introduced me to Jesus Christ and showed me how I could be born again. He showed me that if I took Christ as Saviour, I would no longer be lonely, despondent, discouraged, but that I would find in Christ complete satisfaction. One night, by my bedside, I acknowledged the fact that I was a sinner, that I believed that Jesus Christ died on the cross of Calvary and then arose from the grave, and I invited Him — the Son of God — to come into my heart. Ever since then, I have realized the presence of the Lord. . . . That is why I am no longer lonely.[1]

The way of experience is certain. So the centuries teach. So human biography attests. Try it. Sit down quietly for ten minutes a day for a month. Take your Bible and read it. It doesn't have all He did or said but it is a thoroughly reliable record. It is sufficient and it is dependable. Read the Gospels — without hurry. Let your mind go out to Jesus. Think about Him. Soon you discover that He who knew what was in men long ago knows you through and through. Then you have a choice — to take Him and find life, or to turn from Him and be empty. When you think about Him and let Him speak, you discover some ugly things in yourself you thought no one would ever see or know, and that to have this Friend permanently they must go. When you see yourself for what you are, seek His forgiveness, ask His pardon, accept the gift of His friendship — lo, He comes.

[1] In *You Are Never Alone*, by Lowell Ditzen, p. 146.

What He was to men and women years ago He is to you today. All His followers who have sincerely tried will tell you that you will find Him not a ghost but a Friend, no mere memory but a living, personal Saviour who will transform your whole nature. The very Christ of history who came across the troubled waters of the Galilean Lake will become the Christ of experience who comes to you across the troubled waters of your twentieth-century life, with His soul-rejuvenating greeting, "It is I." And you will know in your own life and learn in your own experience who He is.

He comes where people gather in His name. The promise to be where even two or three are gathered has never been violated. When men and women and boys and girls invite this Friend, open their lives to Him, He comes. He comes if we will let Him come.

He comes in His Church. And the Church is wherever His followers gather in His name, wherever the gospel is preached, and the sacraments administered. I shall never forget one night in my boyhood days when the Church—the body of Christ—came to our home and into my heart. It was a New Year's Eve watch-night service. We watched the old year out by singing hymns and reading the Bible, and my uncle, a college student for the ministry, gave a talk about Christ. At midnight we were on our knees in prayer. Somehow that night Jesus Christ came, searched me out, lighted up the hidden corners of my soul, exposed the emptiness and littleness of my youthful heart and let His light in so that I knew what I ought to be through Him. And when I asked Him to forgive me He did. When I asked Him to fill my soul with new life and power He did. Something deep and unutterable overflowed in me that night. I knew I would never, never be alone again. I wanted to love everybody. I promised Him I would go where He wanted me to go, be what He wanted me to be. Nothing seemed too great or too impossible for this Friend.

Nothing else will permanently satisfy the heart. Our souls were designed for the Living Christ, and when out of Him we are "out of sorts." With Him we have life. And this Friend is the fulfillment of all our desires. His presence, His aliveness, His authentic reality, is the answer to all our prayers.

In the Roman Church a red vigil lamp symbolizes His presence on the altar of God. In our church He enters directly and spiritually. Liturgy and ritual, word and song, are intended to be vehicles by which He comes. I like the cross on the Holy Table in our chancel and the lovely windows with their symbols, so that no matter how poorly I preach, there is always something to lead us to Christ. But too many and the wrong kind of symbols can cramp His Spirit; the instrument can choke the reality. He must come to us as persons, for He is a person. Thank God, He does come. He comes here when we let Him in, when discords are put aside, when harmony prevails, when love abounds. He comes here in response to the prayers of His friends.

Everyone must have his own way of prayer. Let me tell you of my ways. I cannot always call on everyone in this large parish as I would like. My colleagues share much of that with me. But I pray and I pray a lot for our members. I love to sit in a pew here or there or yonder and think of the person who usually sits in that spot — think of his needs, his burdens, and ask Christ to meet that need, to lift that burden. I tell you there is no other place where He comes to answer my prayers as He does here. Try it some time and you will corroborate in your experience what I testify with my lips.

In St. Paul's Cathedral in London, there is an illuminated copy of the world-famous painting inspired by the text: "Behold, I stand at the door, and knock; if any man hear my voice, and open the door, I will come in to him" (Revelation 3:20). You are acquainted with the picture. It shows Christ standing at the door of a man's soul, gently knocking. But the door has no latch or knob on the outside. It can only be opened from within.

Stand before that image, as mankind has done for generations. Respond to its urgent pleadings. Open the door from the inside — the secret place where you live — where is determined who and what has dominion over your life. Resolutely if necessary, gently if that is sufficient, open that door — even here and now — open the door in trust and humility to the Seeker who said, "I have called you friends," and lo! He will enter — and walk with you a way which neither life nor death, nor things present, nor things to come can break.

"Even so come, Lord Jesus" (Revelation 22:20).

4

WHERE CHRIST IS LOST

JESUS was just a boy of twelve when the episode recorded in our New Testament lesson took place. In His home town He was known as an apprentice carpenter who worked in the shop with Joseph. In His thirteenth year, Mary and Joseph took Him for the first time on a Passover pilgrimage to Jerusalem. It is a long journey by foot from Nazareth to Jerusalem. It must have been a supremely exciting and spiritually enriching experience for a Jewish boy with the spiritual aptitudes already conspicuous in Jesus.

The celebration was ended and the parents joined the cavalcade of pilgrims returning through the valleys and over the hills to the villages and towns in ancient Palestine. They assumed that Jesus was among the company. At the end of a long day, when they were about to bed down for the night, they looked for the boy, but they could not find Him. Worry led to desperation and panic as Mary and Joseph hurriedly searched among kinsfolk and friends. Whatever was required, they had to find this boy. They reversed their direction, hiked back to Jerusalem, searched through the streets, the markets, the dwelling places for one day, for two days, and at last after three days they found Him. They recovered Him in the temple — the very temple where they had lost Him. All the time they had been searching for Him He was searching out the deeper meaning of the Scriptures with the rabbis and teachers on the temple staff. Jesus had been lost by people who loved Him best, and they lost Him in the church.

25

The history of Christianity is replete with tales of how men have lost Jesus in the Church. When His person, His spirit, and His love have departed, terrible consequences have followed for the Church. When the Christian spirit has vanished and Christ's presence has departed, the life of the Church has been ugly and mean, and the Lord whom the Church professed to serve has been offended. History contains black pages that tell how men have tortured, murdered, and burned one another when men pretended to serve Him but were unaware of the reality of His presence. Sometimes men otherwise good — frequently dedicated to the Church, intending to serve Christ, but concentrating on the marginal and non-essential rather than the central reality of Christ — have left a frightful record of persecution and martyr-dom. When the spirit of Jesus Christ goes out of His Church, frightful things can happen. Jesus Christ can be lost in Church. Jesus has been lost in Church. But the other side of this truth is that Jesus can be found in His Church.

Let us see how easy it is to lose Christ in Church. He is most easily lost when His disciples give their primary attention to sec-ondary concerns. The first business of the Church is the procla-mation of the good news of the gospel, in winning men to Christ and nurturing them in Christian truth and grace. The main business of the Church is the ordering of souls, the mediation of God's grace and truth to humankind. All else is to make possible the fulfillment of this mission. But sometimes Christ is lost in the methods, the machinery, the structure, and the organ-ization of the Church.

Christ can be lost in excessive concern about spiritual authority. Where does ultimate spiritual authority reside in the Church? Who, for example, are truly ordained ministers of the Church? This apparently simple subject is one of the chief barriers in making any progress toward Church union. Who possesses apostolic ordination? We Presbyterians believe that our clergy-men have been episcopally ordained. What does all this mean?

To us it means that the presbytery, in the performance of its
episcopal functions, ordains all clergymen. The presbytery acts
as bishop. We believe this is the way clergymen of the Church
have always been given the authority of their office. The mark
of ordination to the Christian ministry has been through the
laying on of the hands of presbyters, who themselves were ordained by presbyters. But there are some denominations which
do not regard as authentic our ordination by unbroken succession
of presbyterial orders.

There are those, especially in the Protestant Episcopal Church,
who believe that spiritual authority in ordination is derived from
a person called a bishop. They believe in more than one rank
of the clergy. They assert there are three ranks — deacons, priests,
and bishops — and that only bishops associated with other clergy
have authority to ordain to the sacred office of the ministry,
and only ministers thus ordained have been given apostolic
authority to celebrate the sacraments and to pronounce the
apostolic benediction. They disregard what we believe to be
the early Church's concept of the bishop. According to our view
and according to most church authorities, the bishop, the pastor,
and the presbyter were one and the same person in the early
Church. The words describe various functions rather than different persons. In the early Church the bishop was always the
senior pastor to a congregation. This is what we Presbyterians
now believe. It was only after many, many years that the pastor
came to be known as the "bishop" or pastor of more than one
congregation and the supervisor of the work of more than one
local church.

At this very moment in the history of the Church this subject
is again being discussed. Yet in the Church, whether the plea is
for episcopal or presbyterial, or even, as in the case of Con-
gregationalists and Baptists, ordination is by a conference, there
is only one essential ministry: that is the perpetual ministry
of the risen and ever-present Lord Himself. All other minis-

tries are derivative, dependent, and functional. It is Christ Himself who ministers to other human beings. It is not the magic of any one method of ordination which qualifies, but rather the continuing ministry of Christ Himself in the Church. If Christ is not to be lost in His own Church, we must give less attention to the ways by which spiritual authority is bestowed and more concern to the reality of the spirit itself. However this authority is given to individuals in the Church, it is given to those individuals by the Church itself.

Sometimes Christ is lost in Church over legal concepts and the administration of the law of the Church. Any ordered society requires standards of procedure, else anarchy results. But the law of the Church must serve the Spirit of Christ and not replace Him. In His day Christ condemned the Pharisaical religion which measured man's righteousness by his conformity to written codes. Righteousness was evaluated by the keeping of fasts and feasts, by obedience and conformity to thousands of minute regulations. But Jesus lifted religion from a thing of negative prohibitions and of precepts to be kept to a level of spirit and attitude manifested in all of life. It is a mark of New Testament Christianity that the door of our church is open to any soul who sincerely confesses Jesus Christ as Lord and Saviour and signifies the same by accepting Christian baptism. All else beyond this is growth in understanding and in grace. We need instruction and discipline, but we must be careful that this does not take precedence over spirit and life, lest Christ be lost in His own Church.

Christ is sometimes lost in His Church in the inordinate and excessive emphasis upon statistics. It is possible to renounce the idolatry of silver and gold only to substitute the idolatry of size. Too many of us genuflect before the ledgers containing the church records. Sometimes we are disposed to evaluate churches and even ministers by the bigness indicated in the statistics. We like impressive records and we like to see growth. We say it is a sign of strength and vitality. There are times when I wish we did not even have reports and that Christ's churches were measured by spiritual vitality rather than in terms of a statistical Goliath or a statistical David with a slingshot.

We know that for order and record such things must be, but to make impressive records of greater significance than spiritual reality is to miss the purpose of the Church and to crowd Christ out. There are no small churches; there are no unimportant congregations. In God's sight every church is a big one and every congregation is important. For my part I would rather have a few big men and women, a few great Christian souls expressing charity and magnanimity and Christian grace than to be head of a multitude of people from whom spiritual reality has fled. I would rather be pastor to a company of people who manifest the spirit of Christ in church than to be the leader of a great mob which has put something other than its Lord in the most important place.

Sometimes Christ can be lost in budgets and financial campaigns. When concern is only for larger budgets rather than for larger work, when people fail to see behind every dollar the spiritual reality and broad ministry of our Lord, then Jesus can be lost. But He can be lost also every time a person or a congregation says No to the plea for more funds when answer to that plea would mean more souls redeemed, more lives edified, more human wrecks salvaged. Christ can be lost when His disciples grudgingly give too little and too late. There are no gospel bargain counters. Christianity is the most costly thing in all the world. It cost God His only Son and it costs His followers everything. They are a people dispossessed of personal wealth or fortune. When Christians are truly Christ's people, there are no money problems in a church.

Again, Christ may be lost in liturgy and forms, in the very acts which are intended to convey Him to His people. Stereotyped, mechanical, heartless formulas, however perfectly executed, if they have not His spirit and grace, can cause a disciple to lose his way and to lose Him. Every church has some form. All are formal churches — from Quaker meeting to Roman mass. Some have good form and some have bad form. It is when the Spirit is gone that Christ is lost in the patterns of prayer in His Church.

Sometimes Christ is lost in Church in bad personal relations within the Church. Often people lose Christ because they do not always see Him in His disciples. Some unpleasant encounter leaves resentment. Some unworthy demonstration imparts a disappointment. Differences of opinion and judgment manifested by personal resentment and sometimes personal abuse drive the living Christ away. Persistent placing of undue emphasis on secondary things deprives the Church of the central reality.

Occasionally one says: "I cannot find God real with *that* man — *that* woman in church. When I see such persons or think of them I am filled with poison." Seeing people instead of Him who is invisible and whom they serve, they lose Christ.

There came a time in my own development when I was almost prompted to give up the ministry because of an unworthy and unfaithful attitude of an older minister. But in the end I learned that Christ must not be lost, regardless of personalities. The Church is a rendezvous for all kinds of people — sinners, hypocrites, saints in the making — all kinds of people who know where help is to be found. Help is in the name of the Lord. If people love one another, have faith in one another, love God and serve Him, they will never lose Jesus Christ in Church.

But if Jesus is ever lost to one in His Church, there is only one way back to Him. It is the way of Mary and Joseph. They lost Jesus in the temple. They set out to find Him. And they found Him just where they had lost Him. They found Him in the temple. In the church they recovered Jesus. When they listened to His voice and looked upon His countenance the record says all were amazed.

Anyone who has lost Jesus can find Him again in His Church. He promised to be in His Church. He is in His Church. He called the Church His Bride and in that marriage of spirit the Bride is inseparable from the Groom — our Lord Jesus Himself. His Church is His Body. As God was in Christ in the mystery of the incarnation, so God is in the Church as the extension of the incarnation. The Christian life is above all a life lived in continual mystical union with Christ in His Body, the Church. A man may fail and at times be in rebellion, but as long as the disciple is with the living Body of Christ, he is not only a child of a family that has God for its Father but a member of a household whose table is presided over by Christ. For the Christian, the Church is not merely a group to safeguard him from his own selfish individualism. It is his only home on earth. Apart from it he is apart from Christ.

Christ promised to be with and in His Body forever. Where people are about the Father's business as was He; where two or three or ten thousand gather in His name; where people sincerely and in deep wistfulness seek Him in the temple, He is there — keeping His promise, "Lo, I am with you alway, even unto the end of the world" (Matthew 28:20).

"... They found him in the temple ..."
Luke 2:46

5

WHERE CHRIST IS FOUND

IN the preceding sermon we pointed out that Jesus had been
lost by the very people who loved Him most, and that they lost
Him in the church. We also noted that they found Him again,
exactly where they had lost Him — in the church. In our
generation, as we have seen, Christ is often lost in His own
Church by His own people. But today we have good news. If
you have lost Jesus in Church — if His presence has become
dim by excessive organization, or fussiness, or rude people, or
poor preaching, you can find Jesus where you lost Him. You
can find Him in His Church.

Maybe for some Jesus will have to be found in repentance
and faith. It may be that Jesus is lost because of *sin*. We do not
like this little word any more. Modern man prefers to talk
about complexes and phobias and psychoses and neuroses when
something is wrong with his personality, his character, or his
soul. Modern psychology teaches us that much of the distress
in life is indeed due to real diseases of the personality. Nevertheless, much of the misery, much of the agony of soul and
damage to personality is here today because we do not face the
simple fact of sin in life. Sin is offense against God. Sin is
failure to love God and obey Him. Sin is anything, *anything*
big or little, exposed or concealed, which separates us from
God or another person. If there is some barrier between you
and another person, if you cannot communicate with another, be
in his presence without ill will or resentment, without jealousy

or a grudge, if you retain inside you some unforgiven hurt — whatever keeps you from friendship or fellowship with another person, that is sin. And sin must be expelled from your life. It is only expelled when in sorrow we confess our sin, ask and receive the forgiveness which Christ grants. If anything separates you from another, you need to repent, for whatever separates you from another person keeps you from God. We may be sure of this, for the summary of the Commandments is "to love God with all our heart and mind and soul and our neighbor as ourselves." We can find Christ in Church if we admit we are sinners in need of Him, and if we confess our sins. He speaks the same word of forgiveness He spoke of old.

Sometimes it is said nothing happens in Church. Nothing happens because we do not expect anything to happen. But we ought to expect something to happen if we expect to meet Christ there. Each Sunday the Christian pulpit extends an invitation to confess Christ and to join His Body, the Church, because Christian preaching is unto repentance and renewal.

We know that something does happen in Church. It happened to that man kneeling with one of the ministers at a chair in the church hall of the National Presbyterian Church, weeping over his sins, asking Christ to forgive him, claiming our Lord's forgiveness, and going out with a new peace in his heart and a glow on his countenance to make amendment for the hurt to others and to live henceforth with Jesus. It happened one night with a young woman kneeling at the chancel rail and surrendering her selfish, willful person to the living Person she met there. It happened to that research scientist who in my study confessed he knew everything about life except how to live it — how he had bungled his own life, damaged his own character, and terribly hurt some other people. Then in an act of heart searching, of true sorrow, of real repentance, he sought and received forgiveness and with the light of Christ brightening his being he went out to live as a reborn soul. These all found Him in the Church.

If you do not find Christ in His Church, it is not because He is not there. It is because you have lost Him — something separates you from Him. It is always sin which separates us from Him. And the saints know this fact best. The more aware of Him a person becomes, the smaller the sin which obscures Him. We may be sure we are making progress when little sins keep us from Him and cause us to lose Him. A consciousness of sin will help us find Him. For Christ is the Saviour who came to seek and save the lost — those who have lost the way in life, those who have been away in the far country, sinning against the love of God, or those whose love has grown cold.

E. Stanley Jones, in one of his books, relates the story of a great redemption. It is the story of a successful businessman, married to a lovely lady who was the mother of his two fine children. As he moved upward in the business world and became one of the chief officers of his firm, he was obliged to travel abroad for extended periods. It was on one of these journeys that he became disloyal to his wife. Then he returned home and his wife welcomed him with the pure love she had given him through the years. He became smitten in the inner life and the anguish led to great distress of conscience. He knew he had sinned against the pure love of his wife and against God. He could find no relief from the agony which grew more and more intense each day. Finally he said, "I will have to tell her; I can stand it no longer. But she will renounce me, and I can't stand that either."

Then in an hour when Christ drew near and conviction was strong he began to pour out to her his miserable tale. As she listened and the meaning of it all came over her, her face became ashen and she backed against the wall and cried out, "O don't hurt me, don't hurt me so." Then suddenly she recovered and said, "John, John, I'll forgive you. We will build up life together again. I'll forgive you." Then the man said, "When I saw my wife's pure love suffering on the cross of my sin, I saw behind her the cross of Another — the love of Another whose love encompassed all loves and whose hurt endured all hurts — and I heard him say, 'I'll forgive you — you are forgiven. We will build up life together.'" And He did forgive and life was made anew.

There is one way to find Jesus in His Church. If you are out of His love, if your sins have hurt Him, then come with yourself, with others, to God Almighty. Repent, and accept Christ's forgiveness. For Jesus is in the Church just where some people have lost Him. You find Him right there and you can find Him in a moment, in a single act.

> *Just as I am, Thou wilt receive,*
> *Wilt welcome, pardon, cleanse, relieve,*
> *Because thy promise, I believe,*
> *O Lamb of God, I come, I come.*

And He may be found as a gradual awareness, coming as an illumination over a period of time.

That is why I say in the next place, Jesus is found in His Church in worship. If you do not worship, you will be separated from God. And to be separated from God is hell. The way to keep out of hell and keep hell out of life is to worship with God's people in God's house, for that is where we find Jesus. That is where Jesus promised to be. That is where He is found. That is where we grow to be like Him.

Go into a Roman Catholic Church and you will see a red vigil lamp burning in the sanctuary near the altar. This is to signify the "real presence." This means that the consecrated, transformed elements are upon the altar, that Christ is physically and really present in the elements at that moment on the altar. The Roman Catholic believes that the action of the priest at the altar transforms the wafer and wine into the body and blood of

Christ and that thereafter this consecrated substance is Christ Himself and Christ is to be adored and worshipped. He is "really present." Devout priests have been known to go insane by dropping a crumb of the wafer and not recovering it, thereby having offended Christ Himself. Roman Catholics believe in the real presence.

Protestants, too, believe in the real presence and they ought to behave as though they believed it. The purpose of the Reformers was to make Christ more real to the people in the Church. Ours is nothing less than the Catholic Church Reformed. Commenting on the sixteen-century Reformation, Evelyn Underhill has written,

> The standard of the priesthood was low, the churches were often neglected. In general, communion was given to the laity only at Easter. The desire of the first reformers, here as elsewhere, was not for mere destruction; but for a simplified and purified Catholic worship. The tendency of the changes they initiated was towards more, not less, devotion than had commonly prevailed; the bringing of the faithful to communion at least four times a year, the establishment in the larger towns of daily services and monthly celebrations of the "Great Mystery", the instruction of all men in Christian truth, and the dedication of the whole of Sunday to the worship of God.

Thus we need to complete what the great Reformers never saw completed. We need to fulfill the life of Jesus Christ in the one Holy Catholic Church Reformed. In that Church He meets His people today as He met them in the glory of the Easter dawn long ago.

The genius of Protestant worship is expressed in the title of the book used in the National Presbyterian Church for directing worship. The title of the book is *Common Worship*. Liturgy means the "work of the people" and the worship of the Reformed Catholic Church is the action of the people, the community of Christian believers encountering and responding to the living Christ in His Body, the Church.

An old picture, which used to hang in many a home, especially among Scottish people, was that of a little girl in Church studiously reading her Bible while other worshippers were assembling. The title of the picture was "Helping the Minister." Worship is not a performance for an audience nor is it a drama or spectacle for observers, though the Roman Church teaches that it is a valid worship if people can "see" the priest celebrating before the altar. True Christian worship, whereby believers find Christ in Church, involves the response of the believing community to Christ Himself as He is revealed in the actions, the prayers, the thoughts, and the meditations of His people.

It is "worth-ship" in the Anglo Saxon derivation.

Worship is response to revelation. It is the giving of the soul, the mind, the life to God — and finding Him coming back into life, a life made new by His presence. Ignatius Loyola prayed, "Take, Lord, and receive all my liberty, my memory, my will, my imagination, and all I have and possess." That is the highest form of worship.

"I pray not that thou shouldest take them out of the world, but that thou shouldest keep them from the evil."
John 17:15

6

IN THE WORLD BUT NOT OF THE WORLD

WHEN we gather for worship we offer a prayer which men call "The Lord's Prayer." But Jesus did not pray that prayer Himself. It asks forgiveness and He needed no forgiveness. He said, "After this manner pray *ye* . . . ." It is a prayer given by Jesus to be offered by His disciples.

The prayer which was the prayer of our Lord is the prayer in the seventeenth chapter of John. It is called "The High Priestly Prayer" for in it the Son of God consecrates Himself before offering His life as the one perfect sacrifice for the sins of the world.

The Protestant Reformer, Philipp Melanchthon, said, "There is no voice which has ever been heard, either in heaven or on earth, more exalted, more holy, more fruitful, more sublime, than this prayer offered by the Son of God Himself." Throughout the centuries men have agreed with this conclusion.

Eight times in the prayer Jesus uses the words "glory" or "glorify." To glorify means "to make resplendent" or "to illuminate." He had glorified God. He had made God known by His life, His teachings and His deeds. Now He will illuminate the true character of God and make known His own role as Messiah and Saviour by going to the cross.

The great crisis is at hand. The climactic events are beginning. It was a crisis not alone for our Lord but it was a crisis of great magnitude for the disciples. Jesus faced death upon the cross.

The disciples faced a leaderless future in a hostile world. He prays for them, saying, "I have given them thy word; and the world has hated them because they are not of the world, even as I am not of the world. I do not pray that thou shouldst take them out of the world, but that thou shouldst keep them from the evil one" (John 17:14, 15, RSV).

Jesus taught them how to live in the world and not be of the world. He demonstrated the lesson in His own life. He brought the life of another world, the world of His heavenly Father, right into the life of this world. He did not yield to the sins of this world nor did He employ the methods of this world. In what He was, in what He said and in what He did, He conveyed the spirit of another world into this world.

But the disciples had not attained such eminence. They were only beginning to understand His message and to absorb the new life He offered. They still held tenaciously to their wild dreams of material things, an earthly kingdom and high places in it. Unsanctified ambition lay hold of them and they vied with one another for positions of power, carefully calculating the rewards...all in the fashion of men of the world. These tyro Christians had a long way to go to maturity. They caught some meanings of the Christian life but not all.

Now the Lord pays them a great compliment. In this prayer He reveals an audacious faith in them. Despite their grandiose dreams, their worldly schemes, their unconsecrated imaginations, their foolish longings and blundering performance, Jesus reveals His abiding confidence in them. He says, "They are not of the world even as I am not of the world." In all their immaturity He trusts them. His whole enterprise depends upon these imperfect men. He values them not because at the moment they have a full understanding of the faith but because they have accepted Him as the Lord of their lives. He values them not by their present quality of life, nor by their position on the road to perfection, but rather by the direction they are facing.

These men were Jesus' men. In essentials they were different men. They belonged to Him. They were "in Him" even as He was in God. They were to have a dual citizenship — in the Kingdom of God and in the kingdoms of this world. They were bi-world creatures, deriving life and power from another world but living it out in this world. Although they were only beginners, they were, in fact, different men. He knew it and He gave them credit for it.

Life would be difficult for these transformed fishermen, farmers and merchants. Jesus was sure of that. As He had evoked hostility, so life for them would be lived amid malign influences and destructive forces. But given the aid and grace of God, they would achieve His goals. He prays, saying, "While I am still in the world I speak these words, so that they may have my joy within them in full measure" (John 17:13, NEB).

Here are the rules for the virile Christian. He is not to flee to some secluded nook, away from the world, insulated against the rough and tumble of things, keeping neatly out of the heat and dust of the day. John Milton said he had little admiration for "a cloistered virtue." Neither had Jesus. And while we respect the monastic motive, we must also heed Jesus' instruction that valid discipleship means not insulation from but head-on confrontation of the world.

Jesus wants His followers to live in the world — the real world. It is not withdrawal but encounter that Jesus prescribes. They are to go into the world but the world is to be taken out of them. "I do not pray that thou shouldst take them out of the world, but that thou shouldst keep them from the evil one."

And so after Pentecost the disciples went out into the world, recalling the Saviour's prayer that they should be in Him as He was in the Father, and at the same time in the world but not of it. They lived the quality of life He gave them, sometimes magnificently, sometimes ingloriously. They met the world with all its pressures and powers and it was not long until men exclaimed,

"Behold how they love one another." "These [men] have turned the world upside down" (Acts 17:6).

How to live in the world, to use the world, to redeem the world until it becomes God's world, without succumbing to the spirit and the methods of the world — to be in it and not of the world — that has been the tensions of the Christian for ages.

In response to "being in the world and not of it" men have gone to live in caves or monasteries, seeking spiritual perfection by withdrawing from society. The anchorite, the extreme type of ascetic, appeared first in the third century, and he has reappeared many times since. In quest of perfection, men have exposed themselves to all kinds of hardships. They have had inadequate clothing or shelter. They have worn coarse clothes and sometimes chains. And there was St. Simon Stylites, who spent many years perched on top of a pillar, the original flagpole sitter, who drew a small number of imitators for several centuries. From the lofty perch, under great privation and discomfort, the Stylites called men to repentance.

Many Christian denominations and sects have arisen to express a form of separatism — "living in the world but not of it." Serious-minded, deeply dedicated Christians have adopted ruthless disciplines, rules of self-denial, trying to follow Christ's teaching. Some have attempted to cut themselves off completely from everything in the world which in their view will contaminate them. Some have adopted a form of simple dress and plain living which mark them in a peculiar way. They sometimes forswear the use of jewelry or cosmetics. Some will wear only home-spun clothes and engage only in homemade entertainment. They eschew what they call worldly pleasures. A chaplain under my supervision in the Army declined to go to certain social events, even to a dinner, because alcoholic beverages were present. He separated himself so successfully from the officers and men of the command that ultimately he was an ineffective minister of religion. Catholics and Protestants alike have their extreme expressions of asceticism.

How to live in the world and not get the world inside you is the Christian concern. How to be in the world — in it as a Christian, yet not bow down to it or be swept away by it — that is the problem.

The great Christians have been men and women who, like their Lord, have drawn apart for prayer and spiritual meditation. But they have been greatest when, like their Lord, they have returned to the rough and tumble of life to lift it. The Salvation Army has its "knee drill" and so must we. Do we not become aware of our emptiness when we do not pray? It is not long until other people find it out. A great violinist once said that if he stopped practicing for one day, he knew it, for one week, the critics knew it, for one month, the patrons knew it, for longer, the whole world would know it. This is what happens when we fail to pray. First we know it and soon everybody else knows it. We must get away from the world for a season to be effective in the world to which we must return.

Throughout our country ministers and church leaders have been engaged in a reassessment of the nature and function of the ministry. Conferences, seminars, and conversations have been taking place. There has been much heart searching and soul scrutiny. There has been an ongoing quest for an authentic Biblical ministry which is historical, theologically sound, and at the same time relevant to life today.

Sooner or later every discussion gets around to the common acknowledgment that as today's churches are organized, most ministers are required to spend too much time on administrative details in the parish church and on the promotion of denominational programs. As a result, there remains too little time for their primary work, which is the ordering of souls, study of the Word, praying, teaching and preaching. Ministers are evaluated by the "bigness" of the church and the efficiency of operations. There is an idolatry of statistics, and ministers of Word and Sacrament are assessed by the standards of commerce. Life for some becomes an intolerable burden.

Looking at institutional religion, a few would jettison the whole concept of an organized Church! This would reduce the Church to a miscellaneous assortment of self-directed, informal associations without order, direction or common organic bond. Radicals seem to think institutional religion is inherently sinful and ought to be abandoned, but the Church *is* an institution and must remain an institution if it is to have meaning. How else can there be the "body" of Christ, except there be the Church in some organized form? To keep the machinery at a minimum and the spiritual expression at the maximum is a perennial problem, not for ministers only but for everyone.

To be in the world and not have the world in us, even in Church life, is the burden of the hour. Yet it must be clear that, as matters really are, a minister without administrative talent for guiding, dispatching and delegating tasks is a helpless and hopeless individual. For only as a man deals swiftly and effectively in this area of work is he free to do the creative "spiritual" work that is his chief calling.

Some, doubtless, are overly zealous about getting into the world. They would strip the ministry of all the cultural dignity it has acquired through many centuries. Total identification with the world is insisted upon and this generally means identification with the most sordid, if not the most lurid, aspects of the world. Man's lot is tragic — and there is no debate about that. But the minister who thinks he is not relevant until he plunges into the abyss of "existential despair" and feels the depth of man's hopelessness may stay *in* the depths, lose the note of joy and hope in the gospel, and eventually emerge as no more than an ecclesiastical beatnik. Instead of his getting into the world and letting the world feel the power of the gospel, the world gets into him with all its corrupting and corroding contagions. The mood of the world and the methods of the world can be imported into the Church quite as readily as the gospel can be exported to the world.

Too many ministers today are afflicted with chronic cynicism. Cynicism has come late in the Church. In art and in literature it came earlier. The intellectuals in art and literature have gotten over their cynicism. They remain sophisticated and they are still groping but they have gone beyond cynicism. In the domain of religion cynicism is something new.

According to the dictionary, a cynic is "a sarcastic, pessimistic person." Let the Church beware lest personal jealousy or vindictive disdain of another be concealed as alleged penetrating analysis. Human criticism apart from the Biblical revelation can with disastrous results be mistaken for divine judgment. Pernicious negativism can be more remote from the authentic Christian gospel than the most exaggerated expressions of "positive thinking." Let the Church beware of that cynicism which dims the light of hope which is the essence of the gospel, dissipates power by divisiveness, and enervates the spiritual energy of the Church.

The summons to the Christian and to his Church is to be in the world without allowing the world in; to mediate the grace of God to the world which God created for His own.

Did you ever hear of the Potter's House, a coffee shop on Columbia Road in Washington? This is the most unique coffee shop in town. It is run by the Church of The Saviour, staffed by volunteer Christian laymen and women who are themselves dedicated and specially trained. Here you can get coffee and refreshments, but soon you will be joined at your table by a companion with whom you will presently be absorbed in conversation — about anything — and in the end you will be discussing the state of your own soul. Here the church is reaching right into life — where men live. In the world but not of it. Why not evangelism in a coffee shop as well as in church or by radio or television?

General William Booth once asked, "Why should all the best tunes be left to the devil?" Why should not Christians enter the world to lift it in Christ's name? Many good gifts has God given to the world which ought to be entered and used to His glory. We should not be afraid of life — or run from it. Art, music, literature, the drama, business and work, the ordinary round of things, should be used in God's service.

Christians, all kinds of Christians, should go where people are — to their clubs, their societies, their sports, their veterans orders, their political organizations, and there live out the Christian life — winning men and lifting men to Christ. That is the business of the Church. It is the duty of the Christian.

For health of spirit there must be the principle of alternation. Go apart for prayer, study, meditation and discipline; that is why we have the Church. And what is the Church? The Church is the family of God's people redeemed by Christ, gathered about a table over which Christ Himself presides as Host. The Church is the only true home of the Christian soul on this earth. Go first into the Church with God's people. Then go out into the rough and tumble where all the world lives, and in the sweat and dust and turmoil and sin witness for Jesus Christ. "Be not conformed to this world," wrote the Apostle, "but be ye transformed" (Romans 12:2) — and be transformers.

That little group for whom Jesus prayed did not exist merely for itself, but to tell the world what God had done for it through Jesus Christ. They were to go into the world to influence it, to save it, to change it from what it was to what it ought to be. For God loves the world. That is why He gave His only begotten Son. That is why Christ says, "As my Father hath sent me, even so send I you" (John 20:21).

"The works that I do shall [you] do also; and greater works than these shall [you] do; because I go unto my Father" (John 14:12).

"Sirs, be of good cheer: for I believe God."

Acts 27:25

7

STANDING UP TO A CRISIS

THERE is no more thrilling story of the sea to be found anywhere than the story of Paul's journey to Rome. Like *Mutiny on the Bounty* or *Treasure Island*, it grips and holds one's interest to the last word. From it we derive a profound message for today. It teaches us how to live in and stand up to a crisis.

With some other prisoners, in the custody of a centurion and a detachment of Roman troops, the Apostle was aboard a ship sailing for the capital of the empire. It was to be the final journey in a life of high adventure. During the voyage a terrific storm arose. The mood of the two hundred and seventy-six persons aboard shifted from hope to despair and back to hope again. For fourteen days and nights the ancient little craft bobbed up and down in the wild tempests of the Mediterranean. Wet and cold, hungry and seasick, with physical resistance reduced through exposure, there was great fear that all would perish. A lesser man than Paul might have wished this were the end, since he was at that moment living under the shadow of the executioner's ax. Believing that the ship with its cargo and passengers would perish, the sailors at one point attempted to let down the lifeboats and sneak away in them before the soldiers and the prisoners should become aware of their betrayal. It was Paul, the prisoner, who detected the plot and persuaded the centurion to restrain them.

At dawn on the fourteenth day Paul stood up in the presence

of the entire company and ate some food and encouraged the others to do likewise. What a sight this must have been! Here was a boat-load of once sturdy seamen and brave soldiers now seasick, weak and discouraged, looking at one of their prisoners brave enough to eat and cheerful enough to inspire courage in each of them. The little bald-headed, bowlegged Apostle set his feet firmly on the slippery deck of the ship and amid all the imminent perils called out, "Be of good cheer, men, for I believe God." In a short time the officers determined to attempt running the ship on a sandy beach. In making the attempt they were caught upon some offshore rocks. Destruction of the vessel was now inevitable. All who could swim were encouraged to take to the sea and head for the shore at once. All non-swimmers were commanded to grasp some of the ship's timbers and paddle toward shore. The remarkable part of this story is that not one life was lost.

The man standing at the center of this scene was a Christian — unperturbed, erect, confident about the voyage and certain of the distant future. He called out to all who would hear, "I believe God."

Many of the elements in this episode symbolize the predicament of modern man in the world crisis of our day. We are living in an age that is adrift, when the old moorings are gone, when the old vessels of tradition, the old ship of state, seem perilously near to a grave in the bottom of the sea of time and eternity. Looking across the human scene we see terribly rough seas and we are doubtful about modern man's ability with chart and compass. We have been given the secrets of the universe; colossal power has been placed in our hands; but now we are afraid that man does not have the ethical excellence, the moral splendor, and the disciplined will to guide the human race through the mounting perils of our age. Man has dreamed of Utopia, has longed for the good life, now and then has caught the vision of its reality, but at the moment everyone wonders if civilization can stand the strain without reverting to a pre-civilized state. One is made to ask, "Is this charming, tempestuous, doom-threatened world a madhouse and man's vision of a better world only an illusion; or has mankind a better destination? Is the kingdom of God a valid clue to life?"

Writing in a recent issue of *This Week* magazine, the editor, William I. Nichols, says that changing conditions in our world are stripping away the great illusion which has contributed to our sense of moral slackness and discontent. Says he: "This illusion was the belief that America, following our victory in World War II, was entitled to easy, automatic, prosperous, and perpetual leadership throughout the free world." The editor of *Atlantic Monthly*, Edward Weeks, reminds us that "fear has become a new national characteristic." A new fatalism seems to have come over us and is doing strange things to the imagination. This is not like us, for until Pearl Harbor day we had confidence in our invincibility. Mr. Weeks goes on to say that in addition to the paralyzing fear which has seized us we have made three great retreats in the past quarter-century. First, our attitude toward sex has cheapened and deteriorated. Second, the beauty of our country and its natural resources has been desecrated. Third, our devotion to our national welfare has declined. To be sure, America has moved forward in many exciting ways, but we have also deteriorated until we are uncertain, hesitant, lacking in direction, and almost paralyzed by fear. How shall we behave in this kind of world? If you look at the attitudes of the men in this ancient story of the sea, you get a clue to the reactions of men in crises.

(1) Some of the men on that boat became hysterical. They reached a point during the storm when they could not think clearly nor make a decision. The uncertainty and the tenseness of the situation excited them, alarmed them, and they gave way to hysteria. Fear of danger is a good thing and is given to us by God to alert us so that we may take proper steps for protection.

But exaggerated fear drives men to frenzy and hysteria and prevents them from taking protective measures. Some of the people on that boat were so upset that they could not think nor act effectively. Their minds and their bodies were numbed. They became bewildered, confused, and impotent.

(2) There was a second group of men on that ship. They were not so excited that they wasted their energy in hysteria. They did come to a conclusion. They simply gave up; they lost hope completely. Even among sturdy sailors there were those who said, "Let's be done with it. Let us jump overboard. Clearly it is futile to try to save ourselves or anybody else." This is the attitude of the cynic who is seized by despair.

(3) Then there was a third group of men who were utterly selfish. They would save their own skin, look out for number one, let the others take care of themselves. This was a small group but they were essential to the lives of the other persons. They were the sailors who tried to deceive the others. Pretending to work at the anchors, they slipped overboard into the lifeboats, hoping to get away from the doomed vessel. They probably reasoned that all other persons aboard were either prisoners or soldiers who knew nothing about survival at sea; in any case they were doomed. This is the attitude of utter selfishness.

In the crisis of our age men reveal all three of these attitudes. There are some who have nothing but despair about the future. They can find no idealism, no leadership, no great hope on the horizons of the world. They are confused and hysterical. They cannot think clearly and they are too impotent to act bravely.

There is a second group which goes a little further. They have thought through the issues of our times. They do not always say it but they have really concluded that the Communists will have their way, that the tides of time run in their favor. It is futile to try to resist the movement of history. We cannot save ourselves. There is nothing left but to await the inevitable doom. Act on this attitude and the glory and the luster have gone out of life. Yield to despair in the face of present-day forces and man has already begun the backward trek to his animal state. Yet some live on this low level.

And then there are those who belong to the third group. They are utterly selfish. They have no feeling of kinship with the rest of the human race, no sense of brotherhood, no feeling of justice, no sensitiveness to suffering, no ties of loyalty even to their own breed. Let us take to the lifeboats, let us get out of here while the getting is good, find an island of security where we can be isolated from the storms of life.

Surely none of these answers is sufficient for the age of crisis in which we live, nor sufficient for any crisis which man must confront. But there is a clue in this story of the sea for any man anywhere in any crisis. It is the attitude of the Christian who beyond the tempests and the strivings of the moment sees that God has an ultimate purpose which He carries forward in spite of crisis and even through crises. It was the Christian, St. Paul, who was master of that situation. When others despaired, when some were too hysterical to think at all, when still others would save only themselves, this man, full of strength and courage, stood up and called out, "Be of good cheer: for I believe God." He, too, must have been hungry, fatigued, cold, and seasick but he never gave way to any of the other attitudes. He stood amid the storm, erect, serene, unperturbed. His thought processes and his energies were not dissipated by hysteria or frustration. Instead of yielding to the temptations of weaker men, Paul thought, and Paul worked out a solution. The one man had enough faith to sustain two hundred and seventy-five other men whose faith had worn thin.

Think of what Paul did, what he said and what he was. He thought and he acted. He saw that the men were weak from hunger. He took bread and gave thanks to God in the presence of them all — even on board ship he did not forget to ask a blessing. He asked them to eat. His example was contagious. They were all cheered and took food. "First that which is natural," Paul wrote in one of his letters, "then that which is spiritual." He kept his senses and he made his resources of mind available for the common good. Moreover, he would not be selfish and like others seek escape in the lifeboat. Paul did something in the crisis.

Paul also said something. Many times he had uttered profound truths as in one of his messages, "Who shall separate us from the love of Christ? shall tribulation, or distress, or persecution, or famine, or nakedness, or peril, or sword?...In all these things we are more than conquerors....For I am persuaded, that neither death, nor life,... nor things present, nor things to come, nor height, nor depth...shall be able to separate us from the love of God" (Romans 8:35-39). He stood there that day calling out above the roaring sea, "Be of good cheer, men, there shall be no loss of life. I believe God."

Paul did something and said something because of what he was. He was a man of faith, relying upon something higher than a stiff upper lip or mere animal courage.

There are times when it is important to *do* something, even though it is a simple and very normal act like eating. The elemental needs must be carefully fulfilled in times of crisis.

But it is necessary also to speak and in speaking to say the right word. There are those who can speak only in calamitous terms, can speak only in utter hopelessness and despair. But Paul spoke another word. For him there was an unseen plus-factor in the situation. With all the masculine eloquence at his command he said boldly, "I believe God." Sometimes that is all there is left to say, but if one is a Christian he must say it, if he believes it. And if he is truly Christ's, he does believe it.

The things which are seen are temporal; the things which are unseen are eternal. In every crisis there are always those things both seen and unseen, temporal and eternal. Amid the stark peril of our times the Christian clings to the truth that God's ways are higher than our ways, His wisdom beyond our wisdom. And even though we do not understand His purposes at the moment, we know, we really know as this Apostle said, "All things work together for good — to them that love God" (Romans 8:28). Believing in God is to trust in the ultimate triumph of His purposes — and His ultimate purpose is to redeem the human race and establish His kingdom among men. It may not come at this moment, but it will come in His time by His methods. Even the end of this order is not the end of all things. "I believe God." This is where we may stake down our lives in any crisis — and that means the world crisis of this nuclear age.

Too many people today think the ship of civilization is near shipwreck and that we will all be lost in the sea of time. They yield to despair and act like the frenzied, weak sailors on that journey long ago. But there is the higher acting and the nobler example of Paul. He acted and he spoke so as to help others. He did all this because of what he was. In the final analysis it was the Christian character of Paul which made the difference. And that is the test today.

Are we good enough and great enough in our lives for this hour? This means believing, really believing in God's ultimate victory. Wherever the philosophy of life is wrong, action will be wrong. Wherever the philosophy of life is right, action will be right. What is needed in this hour of crisis is more men with the clear-headed, competent action, spiritual discipline, and resolute faith of the Apostle. With that faith we can make the port of God's eternal purpose through any storm.

When Her Majesty Queen Elizabeth worshipped with the congregation of the National Presbyterian Church, the President of the United States, Dwight D. Eisenhower, requested that we sing the great hymn by Dr. Hugh T. Kerr:

God of our life, through all the circling years,
  We trust in Thee;
In all the past, through all our hopes and fears
  Thy hand we see.
With each new day when morning lifts the veil,
  We own Thy mercies,
  Lord, which never fail.

God of the past, our times are in Thy hand;
  With us abide.
Lead us by faith to hope's true Promised Land;
  Be Thou our guide.
With Thee to bless, the darkness shines as light
  And faith's fair vision
  Changes into sight.

God of the coming years, through paths unknown
  We follow Thee;
When we are strong, Lord, leave us not alone;
  Our refuge be.
Be Thou for us in life our Daily Bread,
  Our heart's true Home,
  When all our years have sped.

Here is the faith that sustains us in life, for it is based upon this ancient truth, "Be of good cheer, I believe God."

*"I gave you a land on which you had
not labored, and cities which you had
not built, and you dwell therein."*
Joshua 24:13, RSV

8

THE CHURCH AND THE NEW FRONTIERS

IN all Biblical literature there is hardly a more beautiful
episode than that related in Joshua 24, when the ancient
people of God were about to enter a new period of national
history. Joshua, their great military commander, had led the
people through many a campaign and the varying vicissitudes
of pioneer life until at last they possessed a land of their own.
Marking the close of one epoch and the opening of another,
the tribes all gathered with the elders, judges and officers for a
solemn act of dedication.

Joshua, speaking to the assembly, told how the people of
Israel had once lived beyond the Euphrates serving other gods;
how the God of Israel had led Abraham through all the land of
Canaan, had given him many children, sustained the generations
in slavery and strengthened them in battle. Now God says to the
new generation, "I gave you a land on which you had not labored,
and cities which you had not built, and you dwell therein; now
therefore fear the Lord, and serve him in sincerity and faith-
fullness" (Joshua 24:13, 14, RSV). And the people responded,
"The Lord our God we will serve and his voice we will obey"
(Joshua 24:24, RSV).

In grateful remembrance and joyful anticipation we, too, make
solemn dedication. We look back, not to fondle a dead past,
but to discover the genius that is at the heart of America. We
look forward to living our days on the frontiers of every area of

human existence. In our forward look we include also a new view of the Church inasmuch as authentic religion has always lived on the frontier.

Socrates explored the frontiers of human reason in his time in the Greek city of Athens and the world is eternally in his debt for his insight and wisdom. Four centuries later the Carpenter of Nazareth, preaching and teaching in the villages and towns of Palestine, crossed new frontiers of human conduct and faith. To a world needing and seeking goodness, He revealed that goodness is not an attainment but an obtainment resulting from a man's response to God's offer of Himself. Holiness, He taught, is not achieved by keeping laws or simply by doing good but by responding to God in love and trust, and our highest life can only be realized when we "love the Lord our God with all our heart and mind and soul and strength, and our neighbor as ourselves" (Luke 10:27). He died on a cross to break through the frontier of man's willfulness, sin, and rejection of God's offer. And after three days He arose.

He was truth. Truth was tortured, mutilated, cursed, abased, put on a cross, killed, put in a tomb. But truth, all that belongs to that reality which is at the heart of the universe, could not be destroyed. There is always a third day and Easter morning when truth breaks all barriers, even death itself, and moves into the new frontiers.

The good news of what God had done in Christ, made known by apostles, pastors, evangelists, and missionaries, penetrated the frontiers of human sin, ignorance, and disease, and set mankind free to return to his pristine state and to move his life upward toward that order "whose builder and maker is God" (Hebrews 11:10).

American life is peculiarly the result of living on the frontiers of faith. It was our spiritual kinsmen, the children of the Reformed faith, more than any others, who exercised the determinating influence at the beginning of our national history. They believed, as we believe, that political freedom is the logical result of spiritual emancipation, that only as men live under the higher sovereignty of God can they be trusted with their own destiny; and that, because this is true, life must be constantly cleansed, renewed, and rededicated for each age.

The Church's place is on the frontier; but the frontier is more than a location. It is wherever any sector of life has to be occupied in the name of Jesus Christ.

The frontier is wherever the life of the Church meets secularism and life is organized apart from any reference to God.

The frontier is wherever the Church meets human ignorance, wherever disease and slavery continue, wherever human dignity is abased and man is deprived of his place as a son of God's redemption and of membership in the family of God. For in our Lord's kingdom every relationship is a family relationship.

The frontier is wherever our life touches the new barbarism. For the new barbarian, rejecting God, and affirming belief in the dialectic of impersonal materialistic forces relentlessly driving man to a certain socialistic destiny, stands outside the borders of Western civilization, flexing his nuclear muscles, threatening doom to all who will not give him his way. In the short span of forty years he has moved from the age of an ox-cart to the age of the jet plane, has added forty-four square miles to his domain every hour since World War II, and exercises dominion over nine hundred million souls in one grand imperial system of thought control, property control, and person control. The frontier is wherever our life meets his.

There is also that barbarian in our midst who rejects the consensus of "self-evident truths" and doctrines about God and man on which America has been built — who depreciates that "ensemble of substantive truths, that structure of basic knowledge," which is the core of the reality known as America. The new barbarian may have the mind of the eighteenth-century philosopher, who neither anticipated nor desired the brutalities of the

French revolution with its Committee of Public Safety, but who prepared his nation for the Revolution by creating a vacuum he was not able to fill. The new barbarian may be the man who repudiates the higher wisdom and judgment of a sovereign ruler of a spiritual and moral universe and reduces all spiritual and moral questions to the test of practical results.

John Courtney Murray says:

> The barbarian need not appear in bearskins with a club in hand. He may wear a Brooks Brothers suit and carry a ball-point pen with which to write his advertising copy. In fact, even beneath the academic gown there may lurk a child of the wilderness, untutored in the high tradition of civility, who goes busily and happily about his work, a domesticated and law-abiding man, engaged in the construction of a philosophy to put an end to all philosophy, and thus put an end to the possibility of a vital consensus and to civility itself. This is perennially the work of the barbarian, to undermine rational standards of judgment, to corrupt the inherited intuitive wisdom by which the people have always lived, and to do this not by spreading new beliefs but by creating a climate of doubt and bewilderment in which clarity about the larger aims of life is dimmed and the self-confidence of the people is destroyed, so that finally what you have is the impotent nihilism of the "generation of the third eye," now presently appearing on our university campuses [and expressed by some contemporary writers].[1]

The new frontier is wherever the Church meets the barbarian. The frontier is wherever science is deified and becomes an end in itself, forgetful that the Catechism is still true, that the chief end of man is to glorify God. Authentic religion need never worry over its dethronement by valid science. There need be no collision nor even competition, for the ends of both are to serve truth. What is true, what is real, and what is of value is true and real and of value, whether it comes by scientific

[1] *We Hold These Truths* (New York: Sheed & Ward, 1960), p. 12.

methodology or by what religion calls revelation. It is only when science claims the methods of science to be the only way to truth and the only test of reality that religion says: "Make way for revelation, the insights of the mystics, and the righteous convictions of the prophets." Out there on the frontier scientists know, as Joseph Kaplan put it, that beyond and beneath all this is something like a great idea reposed in a mind which we in the Church call God. Men of science and men of religion, working on the frontiers of time, are challenged to look without, to look within, and to look up, that there may yet come that kingdom whose builder and maker is God.

There is the great frontier of faith which is bigger and more challenging than any which prompted Abraham when he left his home beside the Euphrates, or Moses when he defied Pharaoh and led the children of Israel out of Egypt into the desert, or young Isaiah when in the temple "he saw the Lord high and lifted up" and then went forth to find God as King of kings and Lord of the whole earth. "Man cannot live by bread alone." Neither can he live by chasing stars or hurling synthetic planets into space. Man lives by the spirit. Whatever else we have been learning about human personality and human life, we now know that man was made for God. God and man belong to each other. Unlike all God's other creatures, man must ever be seeking something beyond and above himself. Long ago St. Augustine said, "God has put eternity into our hearts so they are restless until they rest in Him." This is as true of each one of us today as it has been true in past generations. The Church will always be needed if we are to penetrate the far distant places in geography, in science, life, and thought. All life is adventure, and exploration will not end until life itself is ended.

The frontier is wherever any man remains unfree, wherever man is captive to anyone or anything less than God. For, in the words of Jefferson, "the God who made us made us free." This is the high truth which people of the Reformed faith, people who were our spiritual kinsmen, have mediated to American life and thence to the rest of the world. That is why we in this heritage and with this tradition have such a heavy responsibility.

God calls us as Christian people and as a Church to live on the frontier—wherever we may find the frontier. We must journey not only along desert paths and jungle trails, but in the teaming alleys of our cities. God wants us to be missionaries not only in the community where we live, not only in the limited environment of our home church, but to the ends of the frontier—and the frontier is more than a location. Only as Church members become Christ's missionaries in their several vocations in government and diplomacy, in industry and commerce, in the home and in the classroom, in the clinic and on the farm, will men perceive that Christ is the way, the truth, and the life. Then to the frontier let us go and make encounter in the name of Christ.

Like the people whom Joshua led, we, too, are a people who follow a covenanting God—a God who strengthens the people who seek to know and to do His will, "who has given us a land for which we did not labor" and who promised His followers that He would be with them to the end of the age.

Then let us say with Joshua's band, "The Lord our God we will serve, and his voice we will obey" (Joshua 24:24, RSV).

9

THE INEVITABLE ENCOUNTER

A FEW great and good men make the higher witness; many more make a lesser witness. But for every man there is an inevitable encounter with the living God. A man may accept God's offer. He may reject the offer. But he cannot escape God's offer of Himself. Athwart all history, and in the midst of man's life, stands the Cross of Christ, proclaiming the lengths to which God has gone in pursuing sinful man. In other religions man is seeking God. In Christianity God is coming to man. God keeps on coming to man until man makes his choice — either to live in God's order or to turn from Him and miss life.

Long ago St. Augustine wrote: "Thou hast made us for Thyself, and our hearts are restless until they rest in Thee." There is only one place for the soul of man, and that is in God. Every other place is "no man's land." To be with God is to be at home. That is the way we were created. And if we are not at home with God, we will travel the far, far county until we return to the place we belong — at home with God.

The universe is built that way. Every living thing has its rightful home. The elements and all living things belong where God put them. The bird belongs in the air, the fish in the water, the soul with God. When we see life completely, we know the Bible to be true:

"In the beginning...God" (Genesis 1:1). "God created man in his own image...and breathed into his nostrils the breath of life; and man became a living soul" (Genesis 1:27, 2:7).

The soul that truly lives is at home with its Creator. Somehow or other we feel this intuitively when we are most truly ourselves. In moments of greatest assurance and in times of true joy we feel that we do belong to God. All other times, of disharmony, insecurity, disquiet, and sometimes shame, are times when God seems far from us. Even the moral bully and the intellectual roughneck, the cynic and the secularist, when they are most truly themselves, know that their souls are designed for something better. They are made to be with God. There is for every man an inevitable encounter with God somewhere at some time — in this life or the next, in this order of being or in another order. We are made that way.

Incompleteness, frustration, purposelessness, monotonous rovings must give way to completeness, to harmony, to home-coming. Homesickness is healed by going home. The stream at last reaches the ocean. The nestling is mothered at eventide. The lambs are folded at sunset. The hunter is home from the hills. The sailor is home from the sea. However distant the soul, and however damaged by wandering, it is always at home when with God.

This instinctive hunger for God is conspicuous in those who seem to be running away from God and at the same time seeking Him. When first I was obliged to study that great poem of Francis Thompson, *The Hound of Heaven*, it seemed to me unfathomable. Now I know that Thompson was right. While God is searching for the soul of man, that soul is running away and at the same time running toward God:

> *I fled Him, down the nights and down the days;*
> *I fled Him, down the arches of the years;*
> *I fled Him, down the labyrinthine ways*
> *Of my own mind; and in the midst of tears*
> *I hid from Him, and under running laughter.*
> *Up vistaed hopes I sped;*
> *And shot, precipitated,*

Adown Titanic glooms of chasmèd fears,
  From those strong Feet that followed, followed after.
    But with unhurrying chase,
    And unperturbèd pace,
  Deliberate speed, majestic instancy,
    They beat — and a Voice beat
    More instant than the Feet —
  "All things betray thee, who betrayest Me."

.   .   .   .

  "Ah, fondest, blindest, weakest,
  I am He Whom thou seekest!
  Thou dravest love from thee, who dravest Me."

There is the truth. Man is seeking and yet running away at the same time. He wants God. He seeks God. He knows his need of God. He goes after Him, yet runs from Him at the same time. He is afraid of promising God more than he can fulfill, of becoming more than he wants to be,

  Lest, having Him, I must have naught beside.

This is a picture of so many people today. They know what they ought to be but they are not brave enough to surrender to the One who can make something of them. Instead, they run away. They flee by pleasure, by sensuous satisfactions, by drink, or by tranquilizing drugs. They are miserable enough to detect their need, but not strong enough to measure up to the demands of healing.

This is the destructive tension we see in so many people. They want the power God gives without the morality He requires. They want God, but they want to give gangway to their baser instincts. They want to "let themselves go," only to go in the wrong direction. They want the joy, the peace, the power which God's life would give them, but at the same time they allow the baser drives, the sensuous surges to overwhelm them. All the goodness of life is burned out, used up, dissipated before they come to their true estate. The man who jettisons the moral law misses life. When a man lies, cheats, steals or lusts, he destroys his personality just as surely as bullets and poison destroy the body. The personality has fulfillment and the soul has life only on God's terms.

Yet God still pursues man.

"Man is afraid of being emotionally taken advantage of, of finding himself committed by some choice he will regret," wrote Leslie Weatherhead. He is afraid of some cherished habit, of some doubtful relationship which he will have to give up. Simultaneously he experiences the heights of hope and the depths of a clinging fear. There is an awful conflict and the depression which comes from hesitation and uncertainty. Only God knows how many miserable people are seeking Him yet at the same time running away from Him.

The central truth of Christianity is that God came to man. He took the initiative. That is the meaning of the incarnation. We cannot escape God. He is here. He is everywhere. It is God who is the seeker. We think our search is arduous and costly, but our search is nothing like the constancy of His search for us. It is not the sheep who sets out to look for the shepherd. It is the shepherd who wanders over the mountains until he finds that reluctant, frightened, timorous, pathetic little thing on the mountainside, longing for the shepherd, at home only in the fold, and yet using all its strength for running in the opposite direction. God, the Good Shepherd, knows His sheep and pursues relentlessly until all are at home where they belong — in the fold of the Father's love and care.

We need to realize that God is around us, that "in him we live, and move, and have our being" (Acts 17:28), that He is here not only in our places of worship but in our homes and in our travels and in our offices.

Since his creation man's home has been with God and his soul's nurture requires the atmosphere of the Father's house. He cannot escape God; he can only accept Him. Sooner or later there is for each of us the inevitable encounter with our Creator.

There is no place in all the universe where we can escape God. There is no place where the soul can be safe from God's pursuit. The fish cannot be taken from the ocean and live. The eagle cannot escape from the air and live. So it is with the soul of man. His atmosphere is God.

"If I ascend up into heaven, thou art there: if I make my bed in hell, behold, thou art there. If I take the wings of the morning and dwell in the uttermost parts of the sea; even there shall thy hand lead me, and thy right hand shall hold me. If I say, Surely the darkness shall cover me; even the night shall be light about me. Yea, the darkness hideth not from thee; but the night shineth as the day: the darkness and the light are both alike to thee" (Psalm 139:8-12).

If you think that you can escape the inevitable encounter, be warned that there is no escape. If you think life can be insulated within a secure and comfortable secularism, apart from any specific reference to God, be assured that you cannot hide from God. Of old it was written, "I heard thy voice...I was afraid...I hid myself" (Genesis 3:10). But Adam could not. Neither can you. You cannot hide from God and you cannot silence His voice. There is a Voice which speaks in unsuspecting moments and a Person who penetrates every barrier of hostility, pride, indifference, and willfulness. God is a God of history — of yesterday, today and forever. He is God of our waking and sleeping, of our going out and coming in. There is no place in heaven, or on earth, or in hell, where you can be safe from God's searching Spirit. If He cannot get to you in Church, He will reach out to you in a mother's love, a little child's trust, the loyalty of a friend, or in the quietness of the seaside, the solitude of a hilltop, the crimson sunset, or the magic of the moonlight. You can run from Him, but you cannot escape Him. You run from Him only to run to Him. Sometime, somewhere, you will have to confront Him. You will hear His invitation. If you would have life, there is nowhere to go but to Him.

"If there is a God," says C. S. Lewis, "you are, in a sense, alone with Him. You cannot put Him off with speculations about your next door neighbors or memories of what you have read in books. What will all chatter and hearsay count when the anaesthetic fog which we call 'nature' or the 'real world' fades away and the Presence in which you have always stood becomes palpable, immediate and unavoidable?"

You just cannot get away from God. You can turn your back on Him, but He will follow you. You can close your ears and clog your mind, but He will come. He is always coming. He is always breaking through out of the everywhere into the here and now.

He comes to us as He came of old — by the seaside, in an upper room, at a meal, or as a Voice and a Presence coming across the waters or walking on a highway. He comes as a Person to persons.

God breaks in upon our consciousness as He wills and as He wishes. He comes in His own way and is understood in our terms. We know very little about personality but we know enough. We know it is not the physical substance called a body of flesh and blood, of bones and tissues, of glands and nerves and organic systems. We know it is more than a substance compounded of salt, lime, potash, phosphorus, and fat. This is only a chemical description of that which houses the personality. Personality is something deep, hidden, indefinable, but real. Personality is that which makes you what you are, and me what I am, and all distinguishable one from another and from every other person in the universe. Personality is a composite of mind and spirit, of emotion and will. We understand one another, and we know each other, only when we think each other's thoughts, feel each other's emotions. We get across to others by some reciprocity of spirit, some attitude of life, or warmth of being. Our encounter with God is inevitable when we think God's thoughts after Him, when we stop running from Him, when we relax and simply take Him in.

"Behold, I stand at the door, and knock" (Revelation 3:20) is still His invitation. But He never comes in until the door is opened from the inside. You can want Him, yet not have Him until you admit Him. But He will never stop knocking on this side of the grave. He knows you better than you know yourself. He knows that yours is only half a life until you let Him in.

And when, in that desperate hour or in that quiet moment, you do let Him in, all life will become new. The will, once at war, will be braced with a central loyalty and love. Personality will cease to be at civil war, with one factor trying to overcome another, and emotional energies tugging in opposite directions. Personality, once lost in the jungle of conflict, will find itself made whole and living in its true environment of perfect harmony with God.

Why live with a civil war? Why let inner enemy fight inner enemy? Why allow tension to press upon tension until the soul shrinks and power vanishes? Why let the whirlwind howl through the tangled jungle of your personality when He stands by to say, "Peace be unto you" (Luke 24:36)?

Look at the brilliant young Rabbi from Tarsus. He had everything a man in his day could wish. He had a good birth, family wealth, education, culture, and citizenship. He "knew it all," yet knew that what he knew was not enough. He was plagued with the malady so common in our day. He was many persons in one — a multitudinous personality. He was always aspiring upward but never reaching the pinnacle, never making the full surrender, never yielding to the higher loyalty because life was congested with so many lower loyalties. So many people want to be good, but they are afraid to surrender fully lest God do something radical with them. The culture about them has so inoculated them with a mild form of religion that they are immune from the real thing. All the while there is an agonizing emptiness to life.

It is written that when the frenzied mob had finished pelting

Stephen with stones, "the witnesses laid down their clothes at a young man's feet, whose name was Saul" (Acts 7:58). What a dubious honor! Saul looked into the pain-racked face of Stephen as the first martyr made the highest witness, and heard the saint say, "Lord, lay not this sin to their charge" (Acts 7:60).

Who knows what emotion surged through that young "defender of the faith" that day. Perhaps Saul said subconsciously: "If this is religion, it is something more glorious than anything in my experience." But the next day Saul applied a new fury to his persecution of Christians — breaking into homes, making arrests, everywhere threatening the safety and peace of the Christian community. When complacency is broken, men sometimes react with greater violence. To avoid accepting a new idea or surrending to a new leader, men keep in motion, hoping to dodge a confrontation with the new challenge. Men easily substitute activity for thought and prayer.

In a little while Saul was on his way down the road to Damascus, armed with warrants for the arrest of Christians who had settled peacefully in great numbers in that city. He expected to make a good haul of prisoners, carry them back to Jerusalem where again would be held the spectacular trial and the public disgrace of the new cult. Once more Saul of Tarsus would be honored. Saul was a man both seeking God and running away as he sped down the road to Damascus.

Then came the blinding light. Thereafter Saul would be Paul. There was a voice — a voice he could neither still nor escape. Here was Paul's inevitable encounter with the Reality who is Christ. "I am Jesus," He said to Paul, "whom thou persecutest" (Acts 9:5).

That voice still calls, still wants to break through to come and remake our old lives into something whole and beautiful and good.

Everything in this world depends on your welcome of this inevitable encounter of man with God.

There was a voice which spoke out across the troubled waters, and is speaking now to our turbulent lives: "It is I; be not afraid."

And the last words of man to God recorded in the Bible are these: "Even so, come, Lord Jesus" (Revelation 22:20).